A Note to Parents and Teachers

Kids can imagine, kids can laugh and kids can learn to read with this exciting new series of first readers. Each book in the Kids Can Read series has been especially written, illustrated and designed for beginning readers. Humorous, easy-to-read stories, appealing characters and topics, and engaging illustrations make for books that kids will want to read over and over again.

To make selecting a book easy for kids, parents and teachers, the Kids Can Read series offers three levels based on different reading abilities:

Level 1: Kids Can Start to Read

Short stories, simple sentences, easy vocabulary, lots of repetition and visual clues for kids just beginning to read.

Level 2: Kids Can Read with Help

Longer stories, varied sentences, increased vocabulary, some repetition and visual clues for kids who have some reading skills, but may need a little help.

Level 3: Kids Can Read Alone

More challenging topics, more complex sentences, advanced vocabulary, language play, minimal repetition and visual clues for kids who are reading by themselves.

With the Kids Can Read series, kids can enter a new and exciting world of reading!

Looking
at Wild Cats

Written by Deborah Hodge
Illustrated by Nancy Gray Ogle

Kids Can Press

I spy ...

A lynx

Look in this book.

Can you find these pictures?

 A hare

 A bobcat kitten

 A tiger

Wild cats

Wild cats are good hunters.

They are strong and fast.

Their claws and teeth are sharp.

Kinds of wild cats

There are many kinds of wild cats.
Here are three kinds.

Cougar

Cougars are big and fast.
Sometimes they are called
mountain lions or panthers.

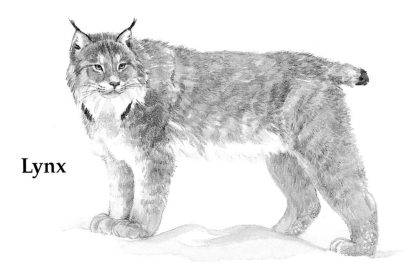

Lynx

Lynx are smaller than cougars.

Lynx have gray fur.

Bobcat

Bobcats are smaller than lynx.

A bobcat can be as big as a medium-sized dog.

Where wild cats live

Wild cats live in wild places.

Cougars live in mountains and forests.

Lynx live in forests in the cold north.

Bobcats live farther south
where it is warmer.

Bobcats like places
with lots of bushes.
They hide in the bushes
when they are hunting.

Bobcat

What wild cats eat

Wild cats hunt for food.
They eat other animals.

Cougars hunt deer.

Lynx hunt snowshoe hares.

Bobcats hunt rabbits, birds and other small animals.

How wild cats hunt

Most wild cats hunt like this lynx.

First, the lynx hides and waits
for an animal to come near.
Look! The lynx sees a hare.

Next, the lynx creeps closer.

Then, the lynx runs and jumps
on the hare to catch it.

Wild cat bodies

Each part of a wild cat's body
has a special job to do.

Eyes
Wild cats have
eyes that see
well at night.

Teeth
Sharp teeth
help wild
cats eat meat.

Fur

Fur keeps wild cats warm. It grows longer in winter.

Legs

Wild cats have strong legs for running and jumping.

Claws

Sharp claws help wild cats hunt and climb trees.

How wild cats move

Wild cats have soft pads
on the bottoms of their feet.
These pads help wild cats
walk and run quietly.

A cougar can run very fast.
Cougars, lynx and bobcats
can swim and climb trees.

A lynx has toes that spread out.

This helps it walk on top of snow.

A bobcat climbs a tree when danger is near.

Wild cat dens

Wild cat homes are called dens.
A wild cat finds a den
when she is going to have babies.

A cougar makes her den
in a cave, in bushes
or under a fallen log.

A bobcat makes her den between rocks.

A lynx makes her den in the forest.
This lynx made her den under a tree.

Baby wild cats

Baby wild cats are called kittens.
Newborn kittens are tiny.

A mother moves her kittens
to a new den if they
are in danger.

At first, kittens cannot see.
They stay warm next to their
mother's body.
A mother wild cat washes
her kittens by licking them.

Bobcat

How wild cats grow and learn

Kittens love to play!
Playing helps kittens grow strong.

Kittens learn by watching their mother.
When they are older,
their mother will show them
how to hunt.

Mother lynx
and kittens

Wild cats and people

Wild cats try to live
far away from people.

Wild cats need lots of space to hunt
and care for their kittens.

Sometimes people build homes and roads
in places where wild cats live.
Then wild cats must look for
new places to live.

Wild cats around the world

There are other kinds of wild cats in places around the world.

This is a lion.

It roars to tell other animals to stay away.

This is a tiger.

It has black stripes

and can jump very high.

This is a leopard.

It can climb trees.

Leopards like to rest on branches.

This is a snow leopard.
It likes to live in cold places
high in the mountains.

This is a cheetah.
It cannot roar,
but it can purr and meow.

Wild cat tracks

An animal footprint is called a track.
Here are some wild cat tracks.

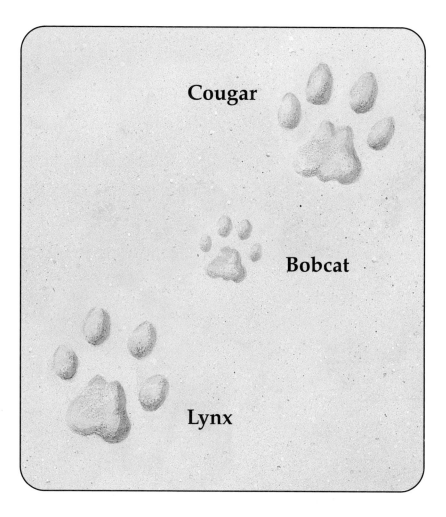

Real wild cat tracks are bigger
than these pictures.

What wild cat am I?

See if you can answer these wild cat riddles.

1. I hunt deer.
   Some people call me a mountain lion.
   What wild cat am I?

2. I make my den between rocks.

   I hunt rabbits, birds

   and other small animals.

   What wild cat am I?

3. I have gray fur.

   My toes help me walk on snow.

   What wild cat am I?

Kids Can Read is a registered trademark of Kids Can Press Ltd.

Text © 1996 Deborah Hodge
Illustrations © 1996 Nancy Gray Ogle
Revised edition © 2008

Kids Can Press acknowledges the financial support of the Government of Ontario, through the Ontario Media Development Corporation's Ontario Book Initiative; the Ontario Arts Council; the Canada Council for the Arts; and the Government of Canada, through the BPIDP, for our publishing activity.

Published in Canada by
Kids Can Press Ltd.
29 Birch Avenue
Toronto, ON M4V 1E2

Published in the U.S. by
Kids Can Press Ltd.
2250 Military Road
Tonawanda, NY 14150

www.kidscanpress.com

Adapted by David MacDonald from the book *Wild Cats*.

Edited by Samantha Swenson and Debbie Rogosin
Designed by Kathleen Gray

Printed and bound in Singapore

The paper used to print this book was produced with elemental chlorine-free pulp, harvested from managed sustainable forests.

The hardcover edition of this book is smyth sewn casebound.
The paperback edition of this book is limp sewn with a drawn-on cover.

CM 08 0 9 8 7 6 5 4 3 2 1
CM PA 08 0 9 8 7 6 5 4 3 2 1

Library and Archives Canada Cataloguing in Publication

Hodge, Deborah
    Looking at wild cats / written by Deborah Hodge ; illustrated by Nancy Gray Ogle. —Rev. ed.

(Kids can read)
Adapted from the 1st ed. published 1996 under title: Wild cats.

ISBN 978-1-55453-284-1 (bound). ISBN 978-1-55453-285-8 (pbk.)

1. Felidae—Juvenile literature. I. Ogle, Nancy Gray II. Title.
III. Series: Kids Can read (Toronto, Ont.)

QL737.C23H63 2008   j599.75   C2007-906612-7

Kids Can Press is a *l'oryus*™ Entertainment company